United States Government Accountability Office

Report to the Ranking Member, Committee on Foreign Relations, U.S. Senate

I0410952

August 2014

FOREIGN ASSISTANCE

USAID Should Update Its Trade Capacity Building Strategy

GAO-14-602

GAO Highlights

Highlights of GAO-14-602, a report to the Ranking Member, Committee on Foreign Relations, U.S. Senate

FOREIGN ASSISTANCE

USAID Should Update Its Trade Capacity Building Strategy

Why GAO Did This Study

Since at least 2001, the United States has provided TCB assistance to developing countries to help them participate in and benefit from global trade. Multiple agencies provide this assistance, which may include support for World Trade Organization accession, customs procedures improvement, or development of infrastructure such as ports and roads. In this report, GAO focuses primarily on USAID because it provided the most funding for TCB in fiscal year 2012 and has a formal strategy focused entirely on TCB. GAO was asked to review the strategy, which is more than a decade old. GAO was also asked to examine USAID efforts to coordinate TCB activities to ensure that the United States is fulfilling its commitment in the most effective way.

In this report, GAO (1) determines the extent to which USAID's 2003 strategy guides USAID's TCB activities and (2) describes methods USAID uses to coordinate TCB efforts with other U.S. government agencies at home and abroad. GAO analyzed agency documents, interviewed relevant officials, and conducted fieldwork in six countries in Africa and Asia, selected for their diverse stages of development and geographic locations.

What GAO Recommends

GAO recommends that the Administrator of USAID update the 2003 TCB strategy to reflect the current TCB environment. USAID agreed with the recommendation.

View GAO-14-602. For more information, contact Kimberly Gianopoulos at (202) 512-8612 or GianopoulosK@gao.gov.

What GAO Found

The U.S. Agency for International Development's (USAID) 2003 trade capacity building (TCB) strategy does not directly guide TCB activities, and parts of the strategy no longer reflect the current TCB environment. USAID's TCB activities are primarily guided by country needs and many of these activities are elements of large development projects that have their own objectives. According to USAID, the strategy's priority areas—participation in trade negotiations, implementation of trade agreements, and economic responsiveness to opportunities for trade—remain relevant. However, some parts of the strategy are not current. For example, the strategy does not include discussion of how USAID should coordinate with the Millennium Challenge Corporation (MCC), which did not exist in 2003 and is a major TCB contributor (see figure). USAID officials told GAO that they had not updated the strategy because they questioned the costs and benefits of doing so given that trade resources were declining and they believed the priorities presented in the strategy were still relevant. However, USAID is still committing significant resources to TCB, and TCB contributes to goals outlined in USAID and the Department of State's joint strategic plan. USAID's TCB strategy may not be as useful as it could be for informing TCB activities because parts of it are no longer current. Moreover, directives, such as those in the Government Performance and Results Act Modernization Act of 2010, can serve as guidance for periodic updating of strategic plans.

U.S. Government Trade Capacity Building Related Obligations by Agency, Fiscal Year 2012 (U.S. dollars in millions)

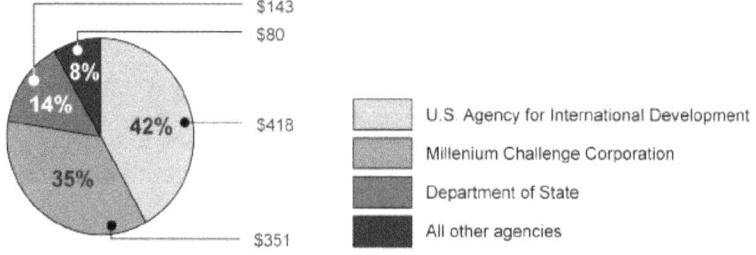

$143
$80

8%
14%
42% — $418
35%

$351

U.S. Agency for International Development
Millenium Challenge Corporation
Department of State
All other agencies

Source: GAO analysis of U.S. government TCB database. | GAO-14-602

Notes: Dollar figures are rounded to the nearest million.

Other agencies include the Departments of Agriculture, Commerce, Defense, Health and Human Services, Homeland Security, Justice, Labor, and Treasury, among others.

The 2003 strategy calls for USAID to be the primary coordinator for U.S. government TCB efforts, and GAO found that USAID coordinates TCB activities at home and abroad using a range of methods, including structured and informal dialogue between stakeholders. Specifically, USAID staff report that they participate in interagency working groups and maintain ongoing discussions with counterparts from other agencies to coordinate TCB activities. For example, at headquarters USAID participates in the Trade Policy Staff Committee, an interagency working group that includes a range of stakeholders and has subcommittees on development and TCB. In the countries GAO visited, GAO found that USAID missions coordinate TCB through formal mechanisms, such as working groups, as well as informal communication.

_____ **United States Government Accountability Office**

Contents

Figures

Abbreviations

CDCS	Country Development Cooperation Strategy
FTA	free trade agreement
MCC	Millennium Challenge Corporation
OPIC	Overseas Private Investment Corporation
State	Department of State
TCB	trade capacity building
TPSC	Trade Policy Staff Committee
USAID	U.S. Agency for International Development
USTR	Office of the U.S. Trade Representative
WTO	World Trade Organization

August 11, 2014

The Honorable Bob Corker
Ranking Member
Committee on Foreign Relations
United States Senate

Dear Senator Corker:

Since at least 2001, the United States has been committed to providing trade capacity building (TCB) assistance to developing countries to help them participate in and benefit from global trade. TCB assistance may include support for World Trade Organization (WTO) accession, customs procedures improvement, or development of infrastructure such as ports and roads. TCB covers multiple categories of assistance across numerous types of trade and development programs that have many goals and are implemented by multiple agencies. Given the diffused nature of TCB assistance, Congress has expressed concern about which agency is ultimately accountable for TCB activities. While the U.S. government is committed to providing TCB, no single agency is responsible for it. We found in 2011 that U.S. agencies provided more than $9 billion in TCB assistance from 2005 through 2010, based on data from the U.S. government TCB database, administered by the U.S. Agency for International Development (USAID).[1] In fiscal year 2012, U.S. government agencies provided nearly $1 billion for TCB activities in more than 120 countries, customs territories, and regional groupings. Given the diverse and disparate nature of TCB activities, congressional oversight of key aspects of this effort, including strategy, coordination, and program management, is important to ensuring that the U.S. government is meeting its TCB commitment. In this report, we focus primarily on USAID

---

[1] GAO, *Foreign Assistance: The United States Provides Wide-ranging Trade Capacity Building Assistance, but Better Reporting and Evaluation Are Needed*, GAO-11-727 (Washington, D.C.: July 29, 2011). As we previously reported in GAO-11-727, USAID collects data to identify and quantify the U.S. government's TCB activities in developing countries through an annual survey of agencies on behalf of the Office of the U.S. Trade Representative (USTR), and oversees a contractor that collects and maintains the survey results in the U.S. government's publicly available online TCB database, accessed May 27, 2014, http://tcb.eads.usaidallnet.gov. USAID's survey asks agencies to place their TCB assistance into a range of categories and estimate funding obligated for each category.

because it is the agency that provided the most funding for TCB—about $418 million—in fiscal year 2012, and has a strategy focused entirely on TCB, released in 2003.[2] In addition, the strategy calls for USAID to take a primary role in coordinating TCB assistance.

You expressed an interest in the current status of USAID's TCB strategy, which is more than a decade old. In addition, you asked us to gain a better understanding of USAID efforts to coordinate TCB activities and to use evaluations to manage them, to help ensure that the United States is fulfilling its TCB commitment in the most effective way. In this report, we (1) determine the extent to which USAID's 2003 strategy guides USAID's TCB activities; (2) describe methods USAID uses to coordinate TCB efforts with other U.S. government agencies at home and abroad; and (3) describe how, if at all, USAID has used TCB evaluations in its program and project management. You also asked us for information on USAID's and the Department of State's (State) obligations and appropriations accounts for TCB efforts. We identified, for fiscal years 2011 and 2012, the appropriation accounts from which USAID and State allocated funds for TCB-related activities and the obligations from these accounts for such activities and provided this information to you in a February 2014 briefing (see app. I).

To address these objectives, we built upon information collected for our 2005 and 2011 reports on TCB and analyzed data from the U.S. government TCB database.[3] Data from the TCB database were previously deemed reliable for our 2005 and 2011 reports on TCB. We identified limitations to the TCB database in our 2011 report on TCB, including that the database did not adequately explain significant factors driving changes in the composition of TCB funding over time. For this report, we assessed data from fiscal years 2008 through 2012 and determined that the data were sufficiently reliable to identify TCB funding by agency, country, and category. Furthermore, in assessing the data, we interviewed key USAID officials and the contractor responsible for administering the database and reviewed supporting documentation.

---

[2]USAID, *USAID Strategy: Building Trade Capacity in the Developing World*, PD-ABX-241 (Washington, D.C.: March 2003).

[3]GAO, *Foreign Assistance: U.S. Trade Capacity Building Extensive, but Its Effectiveness Has Yet to Be Evaluated*, GAO-05-150 (Washington, D.C.: Feb. 11, 2005), GAO-11-727, and the U.S. government TCB database, accessed May 28, 2014, http://tcb.eads.usaidallnet.gov/.

We primarily focused on TCB activities that USAID conducted because USAID provided the most funding of all U.S. agencies for TCB activities in 2012. However, we also sought the views of three other entities in our review regarding coordination with USAID on TCB activities: (1) State, because it is committed to supporting the negotiation and implementation of trade agreements and thereby helps countries advance trade initiatives; (2) the Millennium Challenge Corporation (MCC) because it conducts TCB-related activities that support its broader strategic and agency mission goals, although it does not have a specific TCB mission; and (3) the Office of the U.S. Trade Representative (USTR) because of its role in leading trade efforts. In conducting our work, we analyzed strategic, budget, and programmatic documents describing these agencies' TCB funding and activities. We also reviewed evaluations of TCB projects. We conducted fieldwork in Vietnam, Laos, Thailand, Ethiopia, Tanzania, and Kenya. We selected these countries because they (1) had a cross-section of projects that would allow us to compare and contrast different types of activities, (2) are at different stages of economic development, (3) are in diverse geographic regions, or (4) had signed an MCC compact and received MCC-related TCB assistance. In each country, we analyzed agencies' strategy, coordination, and program management efforts. We also interviewed agency officials, host government officials, and contractors implementing TCB activities in the field and visited TCB project sites. Our findings from these countries are not generalizable to the universe of all USAID TCB activities. Appendix II provides a detailed discussion of our objectives, scope, and methodology.

We conducted this performance audit from October 2013 to August 2014 in accordance with generally accepted government auditing standards. Those standards require that we plan and perform the audit to obtain sufficient, appropriate evidence to provide a reasonable basis for our findings and conclusions based on our audit objectives. We believe that the evidence obtained provides a reasonable basis for our findings and conclusions based on our audit objectives.

Background

Definition and Goal of Trade Capacity Building

TCB is usually defined broadly to include all types of development assistance that positively affect a country's ability to secure benefits from international trade. Such assistance includes addressing

- the regulatory environment for business, trade, and investment;

- constraints such as low capacity for production and entrepreneurship; and
- inadequate physical infrastructure, such as poor transport and storage facilities. (See app. III for a detailed list of TCB category definitions in the U.S. government TCB database.)

USAID's TCB goal is to increase the number of developing countries that are harnessing global economic forces to accelerate growth and increase incomes.

Roles of Key Agencies Involved in TCB

A variety of U.S. agencies have a role in providing TCB assistance. In fiscal year 2012, according to the U.S. government TCB database, a total of 19 organizations obligated funding for TCB-related activities.[4] The roles and responsibilities of four key agencies involved are described below:

- *USAID*: One of USAID's core development objectives is to promote sustainable, broad-based economic growth by helping developing countries increase their exports through trade capacity building. As outlined in its March 2003 document, *Building Trade Capacity in the Developing World*, USAID aims to achieve its TCB goal by supporting participation in trade negotiations, implementation of trade agreements, and economic responsiveness to trade opportunities. USAID plans, funds, and implements TCB activities at both the agency and country levels. According to USAID's 2003 TCB strategy, USAID should take a primary role in coordinating assistance among agencies engaged in TCB activities. In fiscal year 2012, USAID obligated about $418 million for TCB-related activities worldwide.
- *State*: Under its strategic goal of promoting economic growth and prosperity, State has committed to supporting the negotiation and implementation of trade agreements. State's Trade Policy and Programs staff help countries advance global, regional, and bilateral trade initiatives, including free trade agreements (FTA) and World Trade Organization (WTO) initiatives. In fiscal year 2012, State obligated about $143 million for TCB-related activities worldwide.
- *MCC*: As we reported in 2011, MCC conducts TCB-related activities—mostly associated with infrastructure development—that support its broader strategic and agency mission goals. However, MCC does not have a specific TCB mission or strategic plans and goals relating

---

[4]In order to present the most current data, GAO accessed the USAID TCB database on August 5, 2014. As of that date, the latest data available was from fiscal year 2012.

specifically to TCB. In fiscal year 2012, MCC obligated about $351 million for TCB-related activities worldwide.

- *USTR*: USTR does not implement or fund any TCB programs but leads trade negotiations that may create demand for TCB assistance or may result in agreements that create opportunities for TCB to improve the ability of the recipient to benefit from its provisions. USTR also plays an advisory role to agencies with programmatic responsibilities, informing those agencies about TCB needs or opportunities related to trade initiatives or negotiations and needs that might emerge related to USTR's broader responsibilities for U.S. international trade policy.

Sixteen other organizations also obligated about $80 million in TCB-related assistance in fiscal year 2012. See figure 1 for illustrative examples of TCB activities that agencies conducted in the countries we visited during our fieldwork.

Figure 1: Multiple Agencies Provide Trade Capacity Building (TCB) Related Assistance through a Broad Range of Activities Worldwide

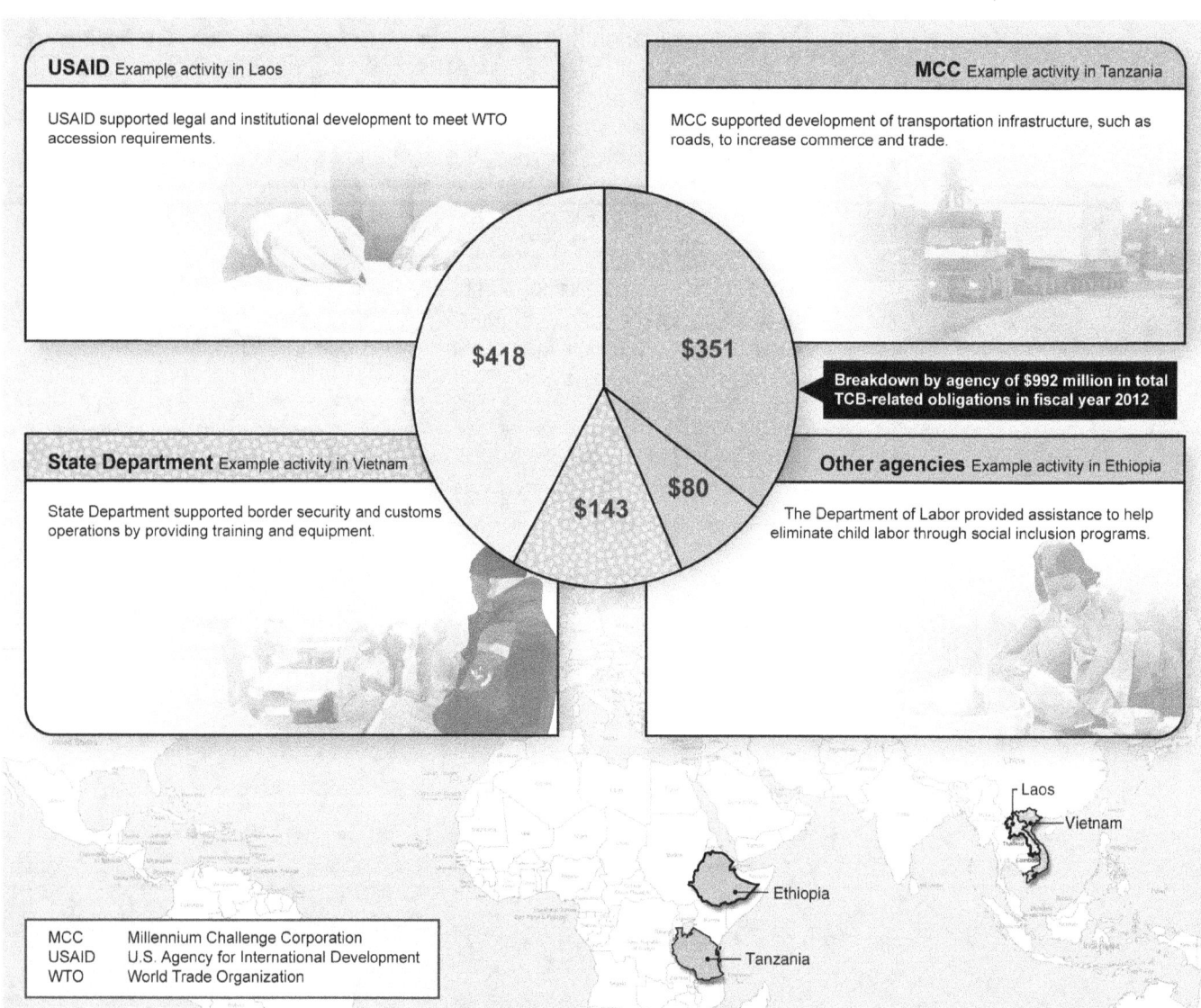

USAID Example activity in Laos

USAID supported legal and institutional development to meet WTO accession requirements.

MCC Example activity in Tanzania

MCC supported development of transportation infrastructure, such as roads, to increase commerce and trade.

$418

$351

Breakdown by agency of $992 million in total TCB-related obligations in fiscal year 2012

State Department Example activity in Vietnam

State Department supported border security and customs operations by providing training and equipment.

$143 $80

Other agencies Example activity in Ethiopia

The Department of Labor provided assistance to help eliminate child labor through social inclusion programs.

Laos

Vietnam

Ethiopia

Tanzania

MCC	Millennium Challenge Corporation
USAID	U.S. Agency for International Development
WTO	World Trade Organization

Source: GAO analysis of agency documents and U.S. government TCB database (data); Map Resources (map). | GAO-14-602

Notes: Dollar figures are rounded to the nearest million. Other agencies include the Departments of Agriculture, Commerce, Defense, Health and Human Services, Homeland Security, Justice, Labor, and Treasury, among others.

USAID Obligated the Most Funds for TCB-Related Activities of Any Agency in Fiscal Years 2011 and 2012

For the two most recent years for which data are available (fiscal years 2011 and 2012), USAID TCB-related obligations totaled more than $1 billion, making USAID the agency that contributed the largest amount during that period. Some obligations reflect agencies' provision of infrastructure and development projects that had trade-related effects—and were therefore counted as TCB—but were conducted to fulfill broader objectives. For example, while USAID reported more than $1 billion in TCB-related obligations for fiscal years 2011 through 2012, the trade and investment program area of USAID's budget for those years consisted of a total of about $348 million.[5]

Over the past 5 years, USAID, State, and MCC provided a total of about $6.7 billion in TCB-related assistance (see fig. 2).

---

[5]According to USAID, a majority of the agency's obligations reported in the U.S. government TCB database reflect activities that are implemented to achieve development objectives other than TCB. USAID's Trade and Investment program area funds, when obligated, are related to TCB and are informed by USAID's TCB strategy, according to USAID.

GAO-14-602 Foreign Assistance

Figure 2: Obligations for Trade Capacity Building (TCB) Related Activities by Agency for Fiscal Years 2008 through 2012

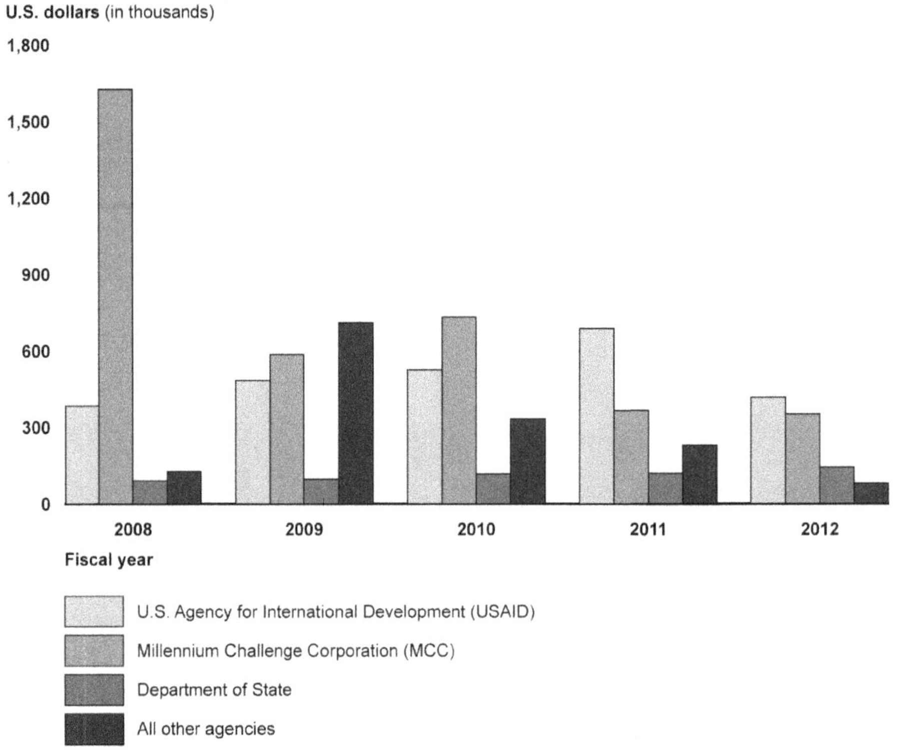

U.S. dollars (in thousands)

Fiscal year

- U.S. Agency for International Development (USAID)
- Millennium Challenge Corporation (MCC)
- Department of State
- All other agencies

Source: GAO analysis of U.S. government TCB database. | GAO-14-602

Notes: Comparisons between MCC and other agencies' funding in any given year may appear distorted because MCC obligates full funding for its 5-year compact agreements in the year the compacts enter into force. The TCB survey methodology captures the amount obligated in the single year the compact enters into force, resulting in large sp kes in MCC annual figures for certain years. For more information, see GAO-11-727.

Depending on the specific fiscal year, other agencies may include the Departments of Agriculture, Commerce, Defense, Health and Human Services, Homeland Security, Justice, Labor, and Treasury, among others.

USAID's TCB Strategy

In 2003, USAID issued a formal strategic plan on TCB—*Building Trade Capacity in the Developing World*—to focus its TCB efforts and guide the selection of new activities. The plan calls for USAID's TCB projects to support the three priority areas of helping countries participate in trade negotiations, implement trade agreements, and take advantage of trade opportunities.[6] The strategy was developed partly in response to the Doha Development Agenda and U.S. commitments to increase global economic growth through free markets and free trade, according to USAID officials.[7] Among other things, the strategy

- defines overall TCB priorities and includes discussion of agency-wide and country-level TCB strategies;
- discusses specific considerations that influence the agency's TCB approach, including labor and environment issues, and negotiations concerning trade agreements;
- provides information on TCB categories and definitions and USAID's TCB initiatives; and
- discusses coordination with other U.S. agencies on TCB activities, calling for USAID to take a primary role in coordination assistance among all the agencies providing TCB assistance to developing countries.

Among the four key agencies that we reviewed, USAID is the only one that has issued a formal strategy focused entirely on TCB.

Prior GAO Work on TCB

In response to continued congressional interest in oversight, we undertook reviews of U.S. TCB activities and issued reports in 2005 and 2011. In our 2005 report, we recommended that USTR and USAID develop a cost-effective strategy to monitor and measure program results and to evaluate the effectiveness of U.S. TCB assistance. In response, USAID in consultation with USTR developed a multicountry evaluation to

---

[6]According to USAID's 2003 TCB strategy, *participation in trade negotiations* includes helping government decision makers to develop the skills to participate fully in international trade negotiations, analyze their effect, and build domestic support for negotiating positions and the international commitments that result. *Implementation of trade agreements* includes building both human and institutional capacities that are required to implement commitments made in the course of multilateral, regional, and bilateral trade negotiations. Helping developing countries *take advantage of the opportunities created by trade* includes support for countries' efforts to strengthen economic policies; remove trade barriers; build well-functioning economic, political, and legal institutions; improve regulatory policies that affect the way firms compete; and improve private sector operating practices and strategies.

[7]The Doha Development Agenda was the result of World Trade Organization (WTO) negotiations begun in 2001 in Doha, Qatar. The agenda recognized that (1) continued multilateral trade liberalization is necessary to accelerate growth and poverty reduction in developing countries and (2) specific steps must be taken to help developing countries take advantage of the opportunities created by trade liberalization.

measure the effectiveness of U.S. TCB assistance that was issued in November 2010. In our 2011 report, we recommended that the Administrator of USAID publicly report identified limitations and key distinctions in the definitional categories of TCB assistance in the U.S. government TCB database. (For more information about the TCB database and definitional categories, see app. III.) Beginning in 2011, USAID streamlined and clarified the definitions of TCB categories to facilitate reporting and improve transparency. This change was reflected in the "technical notes" section of the TCB database.

USAID's TCB Strategy Does Not Guide TCB Activities and Parts of It Are No Longer Current

TCB Activities in the Field Are Guided by Country-Specific Needs

According to USAID officials, development and implementation of TCB activities in the field are guided more by country-specific strategies that incorporate country needs, circumstances, and priorities than by USAID's 2003 TCB strategy. This approach is consistent with guidance provided by the TCB strategy, as well. Specifically, USAID's TCB strategy states that the selection and prioritization of TCB activities at the country level will continue to be determined by missions' country-specific strategic plans and resources. USAID officials also stated that in countries associated with specific trade negotiations or agreements, TCB activities are also derived from the needs identified through those negotiations or agreements.

The main strategy document that guides USAID activities in the field, including TCB activities, is the missions' Country Development Cooperation Strategy (CDCS), according to USAID officials. USAID policy requires most USAID missions to prepare a CDCS, which is a 5-year strategy that serves as the basis for the mission's assistance planning, budgeting, and resource allocation and is based on country needs and U.S. priorities. It is developed in consultation with partner country governments and citizens, civil society organizations, the private sector, multilateral organizations, other donors, and other USG agencies. USAID officials at the USAID Mission in Ethiopia stated that the mission's CDCS is the main strategy guiding their TCB activities. For example, Ethiopia's

CDCS calls for TCB-related activities under its objective of increasing economic growth with resiliency in rural Ethiopia. This objective focuses on strengthening agricultural value chains—the process or activities by which relevant firms add value to a product—by increasing the availability of market-based information, among other things. The objective also focuses on improving private sector competitiveness through efforts such as trade and customs reform. The Agribusiness and Market Development Project is an example of TCB activities in Ethiopia that were guided by this objective. The Agribusiness and Market Development project has activities aimed at improving the global competitiveness of selected value chains for products such as sesame, chickpeas, and coffee, and increasing private sector access to finance and investment.

To help identify TCB needs and provide further strategic guidance for their development of specific TCB programs, USAID missions also use ongoing trade negotiations—such as bilateral trade agreements or World Trade Organization (WTO) accession—and commitments made under existing trade agreements. During our fieldwork, USAID officials in both Vietnam and Laos reported that development and implementation of the mission's TCB activities were guided by needs identified by USAID and the host government during the negotiation and implementation of trade agreements and WTO accession. Specific examples of TCB assistance that was guided by these events are Vietnam's Support for Trade Acceleration Projects (STAR I and STAR II), which ran from 2001-2010. STAR I and II provided technical assistance to the Vietnamese government to facilitate revision of its commercial laws, legal procedures, transparency, and appeals processes to meet requirements under the U.S. and Vietnam bilateral trade agreement and the WTO.

Many TCB Activities Are Components of Large Development Projects That May Not Have TCB as a Primary Objective

According to USAID officials, a large portion of the agency's TCB assistance is provided as a component of large development programs with their own strategies, goals, and objectives. These large programs provide TCB as a means to achieving other development objectives, such as food security, adaptation to climate change, or democracy and governance, and are therefore guided by strategies and policies directed at those objectives. We found examples of such programs in the African countries we visited, Tanzania and Ethiopia. USAID's officials in the East Africa and Tanzania missions reported that most of the TCB-related activities in Tanzania are part of the "Feed the Future" initiative and are therefore guided by USAID's Feed the Future strategy for the country.[8] An example of such activities is the Staples Value Chain Development project in Tanzania. This project includes activities aimed at improving the competitiveness and productivity of maize and rice value chains in Tanzania, and facilitating improved domestic and regional trade.[9] This activity is guided by the Feed the Future Strategy but also clearly facilitates trade and thus has TCB components.

A USAID official reported that because TCB assistance is often a component of large development programs, USAID's total reported TCB assistance deliberately includes a broad range of activities to capture all types of U.S.-provided TCB assistance. The official stated that a large portion of USAID's total reported TCB assistance is for non-TCB focused development projects that have TCB-related effects. USAID officials reported that in some cases TCB needs to be woven into other development projects as there is no dedicated funding source for TCB activities. For example, USAID mission officials in Ethiopia reported that they work TCB into broader agriculture and other development programs because they have no dedicated funding for specific TCB programs.

USAID's 2003 TCB Strategy Identifies Priorities for TCB Activities but Does Not Reflect the Current TCB Environment

The 2003 TCB strategy identifies priorities for TCB that USAID officials told us are still relevant but does not reflect changes in the TCB environment that have occurred over the past decade.[10] The strategy, while not directive, is intended to provide guidance, context, and options to help operating units understand their specific roles related to TCB, according to USAID officials. For example, agency-level strategies, such as the TCB strategy, should be incorporated into missions' CDCS,

---

[8]According to its website, Feed the Future is the U.S. government's global hunger and food security initiative, targeted to help reduce the effects of extreme poverty, undernutrition, and hunger. To achieve this goal, Feed the Future agencies work with partner countries to develop their agriculture sectors and break the cycle of poverty and hunger. Led by USAID, Feed the Future draws on the agricultural, trade, investment, development and policy resources and expertise of 10 U.S. agencies. Accessed May 29, 2014, http://www.feedthefuture.gov/.

[9]The Staples Value Chain Development project is part of USAID's Feed the Future initiative in Tanzania and aligns with the Feed the Future goal to harmonize regional hunger- and poverty-fighting efforts in countries with chronic food insecurity and insufficient production of staple crops.

[10]The TCB environment refers to the context—including all conditions, entities, events, and surrounding factors—in which agencies providing TCB assistance are operating.

according to USAID guidance on mission-specific strategies. According to USAID officials, the priorities presented in the TCB strategy—participation in trade negotiations, implementation of trade agreements, and economic responsiveness to opportunities for trade— are still relevant and cover all TCB activities although the strategy has not been updated since 2003. USAID officials also noted that the strategy is supplemented with guidance related to specific TCB activities and trade agreements. However, since the strategy was developed, the TCB environment in which USAID operates has changed significantly. For example, the total number of free trade agreements the United States has entered into has increased from 3 in 2003 to 14 as of May 2014, and the number of trade and investment framework agreements signed by the United States increased from 19 in 2003 to 50 as of May 2014. In addition, according to USAID, most of the developing countries it has worked with have become WTO members.

It is generally accepted that strategies should be periodically updated to reflect the current environment. For example, according to USAID's guidance, its mission country development cooperation strategies are only 5-year strategies. We also note that the Government Performance and Results Act Modernization Act of 2010 requires agencies to update and revise their strategic plans at least every 4 years.[11] In addition, desirable characteristics of a national strategy include discussion of the current operating environment.[12] Moreover, a multicountry evaluation of USAID's TCB assistance, released in 2010, stated that the usefulness of USAID's 2003 TCB strategy diminishes as time passes and the base of empirical literature on TCB and U.S. development policy evolves.[13] The evaluation recommended that USAID update the 2003 strategy to reflect

---

[11]Sec. 2 of Pub. L. No. 111-352, 124 Stat. 3866 at 3867. The Government Performance and Results Act Modernization Act of 2010 amends the Government Performance and Results Act of 1993, Pub. L. No. 103-62, 107 Stat 285 (1993).

[12]In prior work, we identified six desirable characteristics for strategies. See GAO-04-408T, *Combating Terrorism: Evaluation of Selected Characteristics in National Strategies Related to Terrorism* (Washington, D.C.: Feb. 3, 2004). To develop the characteristics, we reviewed several sources of information, including statutory requirements pertaining to national strategies, the Government Performance and Results Act of 1993, and general literature on strategic planning and performance. In addition, among other things, we studied past reports and testimonies for findings and recommendations pertaining to the desirable elements of a national strategy.

[13]Management Systems International, "From Aid to Trade: Delivering Results: A Cross-Country Evaluation of USAID Trade Capacity Building" (Washington, D.C.: Nov. 24, 2010).

the latest developments and findings on trade facilitation and other determinants of developing country export performance.[14]

Given the changes that have occurred over the past 11 years, USAID's 2003 TCB strategy is outdated in several areas. For example,

- *The coordination section of the strategy does not include all agencies now providing TCB assistance.* The number of agencies involved in providing TCB increased from 15 in 2003 to 19 in 2012, but the coordination section of the strategy does not reflect that change. For example, the strategy does not discuss how USAID is to coordinate with MCC, the second-largest contributor of TCB assistance in fiscal year 2012, since MCC was established after 2003.
- *Some trade initiatives discussed in the strategy are no longer current.* The strategy refers to a number of outdated initiatives, including the proposed Free Trade Area of the Americas, for which negotiations ended in 2005 with no agreement. It also refers to a number of potential trade agreements that have since been completed, including the Dominican Republic-Central American Free Trade Agreement and the U.S.–Morocco Free Trade Area.
- *The strategy does not reflect changes in emphasis placed on TCB priorities.* Changes since 2003 in the emphasis, or importance, USAID places on each priority are not reflected in the strategy. For example, USAID reported that it has placed more emphasis recently on trade facilitation initiatives, such as streamlining customs clearance procedures and increasing transparency. USAID has also reported utilizing fewer resources on the priority of participation in trade negotiations in recent years, conducting fewer activities related to WTO accession because many of the developing countries USAID has worked with have become WTO members.
- *The TCB database categories of TCB activities, included as an appendix to the strategy, have changed.* The original list of categories of TCB activities provided in the strategy's appendix no longer match up exactly with the current database categories that USAID uses. USAID streamlined the categories in fiscal year 2011, resulting in fewer overall.
- *The strategy does not incorporate lessons learned from over 10 years of TCB assistance.* For example, the strategy does not reflect

---

[14]In August 2013, in responding to GAO's recommendations in GAO-11-727, USAID reported that it was updating its TCB strategy in response to the recommendation in the 2010 evaluation. As of June 2014, there were no updates to the strategy.

changes in USAID's approaches to providing TCB assistance since 2003, and it does not include lessons learned identified in the 2010 multicountry evaluation of TCB assistance.

USAID officials in Washington, D.C., told us that although they have had discussions about updating the strategy, they have not updated it because they question the costs and benefits of a new strategy given that trade resources are declining and because the priorities presented in the strategy still remain relevant, in their view. A USAID official reported that the focus in recent years had been on supporting ongoing field programs and that these efforts took precedence over updating the TCB strategy. USAID officials also reported that they believe an update to the existing strategy would have limited impact, largely serving to maintain the status quo, since the priorities have remained the same and all activities still fit under the strategy. However, we previously found that assessing the current environment has a critical impact on the success of strategic planning.[15] Further, even though USAID reports that trade resources are declining, it continues to commit significant resources, obligating over $1 billion for TCB-related activities in fiscal years 2011 and 2012. TCB also contributes to meeting goals outlined in USAID and State's Joint Strategic Plan.[16]

Given the changes in the TCB environment since 2003, updating the strategy to reflect those changes could put USAID missions in a better position to select and implement TCB activities. Moreover, an updated strategy could provide USAID missions with important information on changing priorities and lessons learned from evaluations and other assessments, which could also help guide their investments in TCB activities. The outdated nature of some parts of the strategy and the fact that it was released over 10 years ago may also limit its use. Multiple

---

[15]In a report on strategic planning, we found that for the planning to be effective, three practices are critical. Organizations must (1) involve their stakeholders, (2) assess their internal and external environments, and (3) align their activities, core processes, and resources to support mission-related outcomes. See *Agencies' Strategic Plans Under GPRA: Key Questions to Facilitate Congressional Review*, GAO/GGD-10.1.16 (Washington, D.C.: May 1997).

[16]In USAID and State's fiscal years 2014-2017 Joint Strategic Plan, TCB activities are being used to help achieve both objectives under the strategic goal of strengthening America's economic reach and positive economic impact. The objectives are (1) to expand access to future markets, investments, and trade; and (2) to promote inclusive economic growth, reduce extreme poverty, and improve food security.

USAID officials we met with in the field were not aware that the strategy existed and did not use it. The number of agencies involved in TCB, and its crosscutting nature, calls for collaboration and coordination to ensure that TCB assistance is meeting U.S. objectives. A USAID official reported that USAID involved relevant agencies in the development of the 2003 TCB strategy to achieve interagency buy-in. However, several other agencies, primarily MCC, have since begun providing TCB assistance. In the absence of an updated strategy, these agencies may be less aware of USAID's TCB priorities and may miss opportunities to leverage resources and ensure that their activities complement USAID's efforts.

USAID Uses Various Methods to Coordinate Trade Capacity Building Activities with Other Agencies

At Headquarters, USAID Participates in Coordinating Bodies and Uses Informal Dialogue to Coordinate TCB Activities

The 2003 strategy calls for USAID to be the primary coordinator for U.S. government TCB efforts, and we found that USAID headquarters staff participate in coordinating bodies, such as interagency working groups, and maintain ongoing discussions with relevant counterparts to coordinate TCB activities. One coordinating body USAID uses is the Trade Policy Staff Committee (TPSC), a USTR-chaired interagency working group that includes a broad range of stakeholders, meets multiple times a year, and has subcommittees focused on development and TCB. According to a USTR official, the TPSC's subcommittees provide channels for USAID to identify developing country trade capacity needs and opportunities. For example, USAID participates in the TPSC Development and Trade Capacity subcommittee, which focuses on topics such as WTO policy and agreements. In this forum, USAID may discuss needs associated with WTO accession with USTR and other agencies to see if an acceding developing country needs help understanding or meeting requirements. The subcommittee communicates informally and meets on an ad hoc basis, but USAID relies on it as a vehicle to identify ways agencies can leverage TCB resources, according to officials.

The USAID Standards Alliance is an example of project-level coordination. The Alliance involves U.S. government trade and regulatory agencies, as well as the private sector, to address trade barriers. Officially introduced in November 2012, the Standards Alliance is a public-private partnership between USAID and the American National Standards Institute, a private non-profit organization whose membership is made up of businesses, professional societies, trade associations, standards developers, and consumer and labor organizations. The Alliance provides capacity-building assistance to developing countries specifically related to the implementation of the WTO Technical Barriers to Trade Agreement. According to USAID, assistance aims to help developing countries improve the quality and safety of the products they export abroad and increase exports, while reducing costs and bureaucratic hurdles. In addition, Standards Alliance activities are implemented in collaboration with USTR and draw heavily on expertise and technical support from other U.S. agencies including the Department of Commerce/National Institute of Standards and Technology and the Consumer Product Safety Commission. In 2013, USAID worked with the Standards Alliance to conduct workshops in Peru that brought together industry representatives and government officials to discuss U.S. and Peruvian experiences and perspectives related to standardization and regulatory practices. About 130 individuals took part in the event, representing a mix of stakeholders in government, industry, testing and certification bodies, and academia.

USAID also reports using other mechanisms, such as shared management structures and cross-agency agreements, to facilitate TCB coordination. For example, the Administrator of USAID sits on the MCC Board of Directors and contributes to the approval of MCC compacts. According to USAID officials, this shared management structure is intended to ensure stakeholder involvement and provides an opportunity to leverage resources on TCB matters. In addition, USAID is represented on the board of the Overseas Private Investment Corporation (OPIC) and contributes to the approval of OPIC deals, which may have TCB-related components.[17] The USAID Office of Development Credit and OPIC also

---

[17] OPIC is a U.S. government development finance institution that provides investors with financing, guarantees, and political risk insurance, among other things. In pursuit of its mission objectives, OPIC at times supports TCB-related activities. For example, in 2012, OPIC supported a project designed to provide loans to agricultural cooperatives in 42 countries for the production and export of commodities such as bananas, cocoa, and coffee.

hold quarterly meetings to discuss project plans and other issues of relevance to both units to help ensure relevant skills and expertise are being utilized for TCB and other activities, according to USAID. In addition to shared management structures, a USAID official reported that it has agreements and works with other agencies that play relatively small roles in TCB, such as the Trade and Development Agency and the Departments of Justice and Labor. Involving stakeholders in this way facilitates leveraging TCB resources, according to a USAID official. For example, in Bangladesh, USAID and the Department of Labor are cooperating on implementation of a program to improve labor conditions, promote independent and democratic labor unions, and support labor rights and worker representation. Such activities fall in line with USAID's TCB objective to address labor issues related to trade and to leverage expertise from across the U.S. government.

In addition to using mechanisms that facilitate coordination, officials at USAID, State, and USTR, told us that they discuss TCB matters frequently and on an ad hoc basis, particularly at the staff level. As TCB needs, opportunities, or issues arise, relevant stakeholders communicate informally to coordinate, according to a USTR official. For example, State's Office of Multilateral Trade Affairs monitors trade-related activities and considers how State could help with TCB. The office coordinates with USAID and USTR counterparts and may suggest TCB opportunities related to free trade agreement (FTA) negotiations or WTO obligations in certain countries, according to a State official. A USTR official also told us that USTR shares its annual TCB priorities with USAID and State using an unofficial document that outlines an inventory of possible efforts. This document provides a notional framework that facilitates informal dialogue and stakeholder involvement.

Abroad, USAID Uses Formal Mechanisms and Informal Dialogue with Stakeholders to Coordinate TCB Activities

In countries we visited, including Ethiopia, Tanzania, Vietnam, and Laos, we found that USAID uses certain formal mechanisms, such as working groups, and informal dialogue with stakeholders to coordinate TCB. According to officials we met, in most locations, USAID participates in a formal embassy working group that addresses TCB matters and involves a range of stakeholders, sometimes including the Chief of Mission. Specifically, in countries we visited, we found the following:

- *Ethiopia.* According to officials we met with, USAID coordinates TCB activities primarily through the Economic Growth and Development working group, which meets monthly. This interagency group, one of five created about a year ago under an ambassadorial directive to address the highest-level embassy priorities, covers TCB matters and related topics, such as WTO accession progress and upcoming visits of U.S. government or private sector personnel. Generally, the Chief of Mission and the USAID Mission Director or their deputies report that they attend the meeting, along with representatives from the Foreign Agricultural Service, USAID, and State. Embassy officials told us that this formal channel, along with frequent informal communication among stakeholders, helps ensure a whole-of-government approach to TCB.

- *Tanzania*. According to officials we met with, USAID and its counterparts discuss TCB and development issues at the embassy's biweekly Governance and Prosperity Working Group. The group includes participants from State, USAID, and MCC, and covers ongoing TCB initiatives and development issues. USAID and relevant agencies also may discuss TCB at the embassy's Power Africa working group, a regular meeting that focuses on power and energy sector projects, which may have trade-related effects such as improving competitiveness or capacity.[18] Officials told us that informal communication about TCB matters occurs frequently on an ad hoc basis as well, helping to ensure that resources and expertise across agencies are fully leveraged.

- *Vietnam*. According to officials we met with, the main mechanism through which TCB is coordinated is the interagency commercial task force, which convenes stakeholders from USAID, State, and other relevant agencies weekly. The embassy Deputy Chief of Mission sets the agenda for the task force and participants provide updates on active projects, issues, and policy considerations related to TCB and commercial activities. According to embassy officials, TCB is a key embassy priority and requires a broad range of engagement with the host government, so coordination is critical. In addition, these officials noted that USAID and its counterparts interact frequently and maintain good working relationships, providing an appropriate environment to enable stakeholders to leverage the range of TCB resources at the embassy.

- *Laos*. According to officials we met with, USAID coordinates its TCB activities in Laos from its regional office in Thailand. USAID does not have a mission in Laos, although it does have a USAID representative (a U.S. Personal Services Contractor) located in the U.S. embassy in

---

[18]Announced in June 2013 by the President of the United States, Power Africa is an initiative to double access to power in sub-Saharan Africa. Initial partner countries include Ethiopia, Ghana, Kenya, Liberia, Nigeria, and Tanzania.

Laos who helps to coordinate USAID regional and bilateral projects, including TCB activities. According to a USAID official, TCB efforts in Laos are relatively small and focused, so formal coordination structures are not necessary or practical. Instead, this official explained that the USAID representative regularly liaises with the State Economics Officer, who meets with the Ambassador weekly. Although no official working group has been established, the Economic Officer, Ambassador, and USAID representative meet at least quarterly to discuss TCB assistance. These discussions help to ensure conflicts are avoided and resources are used effectively. Because economic development and TCB projects have been key priorities of the embassy in Laos in recent years, USAID communicates frequently with State counterparts in-country, according to an official. In addition, another official told us that USAID and State worked together to develop the Integrated Country Strategy for Laos, helping to ensure that TCB fit into a common set of interagency goals and priorities.

USAID Has Taken Steps to Use Evaluations in Its Management of TCB Activities

At the Headquarters Level, USAID Has Introduced a Web-based Tool and Taken Other Actions in Response to its 2010 Evaluation

At the headquarters level, USAID officials noted that they have introduced a web-based tool and taken various actions, such as committing to regularly identify best practices, based on the multicountry evaluation completed in 2010. In 2013, USAID launched a web-based tool, called "Project Starter," designed to bring together guidance, templates, examples, and checklists to facilitate monitoring, evaluation, and adaptive learning in TCB activities. From January 1, 2014, through March 31, 2014, the Project Starter website had nearly 4,000 visitors, including a mix of technical, program, and managerial staff from headquarters and the field.

In our 2011 report, we found that USAID had commissioned a limited number of evaluations of TCB programs to assess long-term results, in part because of the resources required and the difficulty of evaluating impact in the area of TCB. We recommended that USAID develop a written plan for using the 2010 multicountry evaluation and conduct further evaluations on an ongoing basis. As a result of our recommendation, USAID committed to conduct every 5 years an analysis of evaluations completed by missions, to identify best practices for trade projects. However, USAID has not incorporated lessons learned identified in the 2010 multicountry evaluation into its TCB strategy.

USAID officials at headquarters also told us that they provide guidance to field staff to facilitate TCB program management, leveraging best practices and lessons learned from evaluations and experience. For example, subject matter experts at headquarters regularly respond to requests for assistance from field staff on designing or evaluating projects. In addition, headquarters staff helped in the design and award of TCB activities in Jordan, Laos, Ghana, Afghanistan, Tanzania, Nigeria, Pakistan, and USAID regional missions in Thailand and West Africa. These activities account for approximately 60 percent of USAID fiscal year 2013 trade funds, according to USAID. In addition, headquarters officials report they provided support for evaluations, results frameworks, and strategy development, to field staff in Morocco, Liberia, West Bank-Gaza, Kenya, and South Africa.

Abroad, USAID Field Staff Have Used Evaluations to Manage Projects at the Country Level

Abroad, USAID field staff have used evaluations and assessments of projects to manage current and future TCB efforts in the countries we visited. During fieldwork, we found that USAID field staff had conducted evaluations and assessments of specific activities and used the information to make changes to ongoing or planned projects as follows:

- *Ethiopia.* USAID conducted a cost-benefit analysis of its support for agricultural value chain projects in 2012, designed to improve productivity and efficiency, among other things. USAID officials told us that based on the analysis, they changed the investment allocation while projects were under way to favor those with better potential for results. In addition, USAID's Ethiopia CDCS calls for elevating the role of evaluations and impact assessments as learning tools throughout the project cycle for continuous updating and promotion of best practices. Officials indicated that the CDCS is the central guiding document for USAID TCB and other activities in-country and that, in accordance with this directive, continuous improvement processes are part of regular operations.
- *Tanzania.* In 2011, USAID's East Africa Trade Hub in Kenya—a regional mission that plays a significant role in managing TCB projects in Tanzania—conducted an assessment of its activities and made changes as a result, according to an official. For example, the

assessment recommended that the Trade Hub work with the embassies in the countries it covers, including Tanzania, to develop a shared vision and to facilitate mutually beneficial relationships. According to a USAID official, the Trade Hub responded by taking steps to address this issue. Specifically, the Trade Hub committed to send a person to visit each embassy in the region at least once a year to discuss goals and priorities, and it provided additional country-specific information on its website so stakeholders could see and monitor its activities anytime. The assessment also recommended that the Trade Hub shift to assisting the East Africa Community, a regional economic group that includes Tanzania, and national authorities with the implementation of policies and procedures. As a result, the Trade Hub reallocated some of its TCB resources away from supporting trade-related business development activities to supporting the East Africa Community, its five members, and regional trade associations focused on regional policy implementation, according to a USAID official.

- *Vietnam.* USAID conducted a performance evaluation of STAR, its main TCB activity, in 2011. One of the evaluation's recommendations was that USAID should focus its future efforts on trade facilitation activities, such as improving customs, transportation, and the commercial regulatory environment. According to the evaluation, this would benefit the trading community and help the host government implement and enforce some of the legal and regulatory reforms put in place over recent years with the support of STAR. A USAID official told us that in response to the recommendation, they designed TCB activities to focus on leveraging relationships with the host government's customs ministry. Specifically, they targeted support toward streamlining customs procedures and regulations with the aim of helping the government and business build on prior reforms. A USAID official also told us that one lesson learned over the years was that involving multiple host government ministries in TCB projects may slow progress. To address this weakness, USAID shifted its approach to focus on a limited number of areas with committed stakeholders while maintaining an ad hoc mechanism for other ministries as needs and opportunities arise.

- *Laos.* Because USAID does not have a presence in Laos, officials told us that they regularly monitor TCB activities in Laos from the regional office in Thailand, working in close coordination with the USAID representative in Laos and embassy staff. They also indicated that early TCB work in Laos focused on establishing a basic legal framework to meet WTO requirements, but as a result of monitoring and evaluating progress, USAID shifted the focus of assistance to facilitating implementation of the laws and regulations put in place. A

USAID official also told us that this year they are updating a Lao Business and Commercial Law and Institutional Reform assessment that will provide a baseline for the new TCB assistance for Laos.

Conclusions

The U.S. government continues to demonstrate a commitment to providing TCB for developing countries, and over the years multiple U.S. agencies have provided this assistance across numerous types of trade and development programs. Given the diffused nature of TCB assistance, Congress has expressed concern about which agency is ultimately accountable for TCB activities. While no single agency is responsible for this type of assistance, USAID has a 2003 TCB strategy that defines overall TCB priorities and discusses coordination with other U.S. agencies. In addition, in fiscal year 2012, USAID provided about $418 million for TCB, the most funding of any U.S. government agency. Therefore, it is important that USAID's strategy reflect the current TCB environment. USAID officials asserted that the priorities in the strategy are still relevant, but we observed that neither USAID nor other agency officials we met with in the field used, or in some cases even knew about, the strategy. Moreover, we found that the strategy may not be as useful as it could be because it is outdated in several areas. For example, the coordination section of the strategy does not include all agencies now providing TCB assistance, the trade initiatives discussed in the strategy are no longer current, and the categories of TCB activities identified in the strategy have changed. Updating the strategy to reflect the current TCB environment would provide USAID an opportunity to examine its TCB priorities in light of changes to the environment and ensure that the priorities are indeed still relevant. A strategy update would also raise awareness of the agency's TCB priorities in relevant missions and offices. In the absence of a government-wide TCB strategy, an effort to update the USAID TCB strategy could also bring together other agencies involved in providing TCB assistance, helping to ensure interagency buy-in on current TCB priorities and goals.

Recommendation for Executive Action

To help ensure that USAID's 2003 TCB strategy is as useful as it could be for informing TCB activities, we recommend that the Administrator of USAID update the strategy to reflect the current TCB environment.

Agency Comments and Our Evaluation

We requested comments on a draft of this report from the Administrator of USAID, the Secretary of State, the Chief Executive Officer of the Millennium Challenge Corporation, and the U.S. Trade Representative.

On July 15, 2014, USAID indicated via e-mail that it agreed with the recommendation and intended to explore options for providing additional guidance to operating units. USAID further indicated that the additional guidance might take the form of drafting a new TCB strategy, updating or amending the old strategy, issuing a separate policy paper, contributing to a broader U.S. government-wide strategy, or some other type of guidance. In its written comments, reproduced in appendix IV, MCC stated that it was in the process of updating the MCC data in the U.S. government TCB database. We did not receive comments from State or USTR.

As agreed with your office, unless you publicly announce the contents of this report earlier, we plan no further distribution until 30 days from the report date. At that time, we will send copies of this report to the appropriate congressional committees, the Administrator of USAID, the Secretary of State, the Chief Executive Officer of the Millennium Challenge Corporation, the U.S. Trade Representative, and other interested parties. In addition, this report is available at no charge on the GAO website at http://www.gao.gov.

If you or your staff have any questions about this report, please contact me at (202) 512-8612 or GianopoulosK@gao.gov. Contact points for our Offices of Congressional Relations and Public Affairs may be found on the last page of this report. GAO staff who made key contributions to this report are listed in appendix V.

Sincerely yours,

Kimberly Gianopoulos
Acting Director, International Affairs and Trade

Appendix I: USAID and State Trade Capacity Building Funding Data, Fiscal Years 2011 through 2012

In fiscal years 2011 through 2012, the U.S. Agency for International Development (USAID) and the Department of State (State) together obligated a total of approximately $1.36 billion for trade capacity building (TCB) related activities. Of that amount, USAID obligated approximately $1.1 billion with funds from seven different accounts. State obligated the approximately $262 million remaining, with funds from seven funding accounts. (See table 1 below.) USAID officials noted that there is no dedicated funding account or directive for TCB activities. USAID officials also noted that the majority of the TCB assistance reported in the database are obligations for development projects that had trade-related effects—and were therefore counted as TCB—but were conducted to fulfill other development objectives.

Table 1: USAID and State Obligations for Trade Capacity Building Related Activities by Funding Account, Fiscal Years 2011 through 2012

Funding agency and account	2011	2012
U.S. Agency for International Development		
Assistance for Eastern Europe and the Baltic States	$350,000	$1,900,000
Assistance for Europe, Eurasia, and Central Asia	$60,269,640	$29,243,598
Assistance for the Independent States of the Former Soviet Union	$5,371,030	$5,495,820
Development Assistance	$292,365,424	$173,071,344
Development Credit Authority, United States	$604,608	-
Economic Support Fund	$327,630,138	$206,397,931
Sub-Saharan Africa, Development Assistance	-	$1,900,000
Total (U.S. Agency for International Development)	**$686,590,840**	**$418,008,693**
Department of State		
Democracy Fund, Department of State	$448,000	-
Educational and Cultural Exchange Programs, Department of State	$43,929,157	$56,652,219
Global Health and Child Survival	-	$690,000
International Organizations and Programs	$20,059,207	$18,847,889
International Narcotics Control and Law Enforcement[a]	$3,904,091	$5,219,385
Iraq Relief and Reconstruction Fund, Executive Office of the President[a]	$61,902	-
Nonproliferation, Anti-Terrorism, Demining and Related Programs[a]	$50,999,493	$61,545,538
Total (Department of State)	**$119,401,850**	**$142,955,031**
Total (Both USAID and State)	**$805,992,690**	**$560,963,724**

Legend: USAID = U.S. Agency for International Development, State = Department of State.

Source: USA D. | GAO-14-602

[a]According to USAID, the International Narcotics Control and Law Enforcement, Department of State; Iraq Relief and Reconstruction Fund, Executive Office of the President; and Nonproliferation, Anti-Terrorism, Demining and Related Programs, Department of State are funding accounts under the Executive Office of the President that are assigned to the Department of State, as State largely manages the funds in these accounts and is responsible for reporting on them.

Appendix II: Objectives, Scope, and Methodology

Our objectives were to (1) determine the extent to which the U.S. Agency for International Development's (USAID) 2003 strategy guides USAID's trade capacity building (TCB) activities; (2) describe methods USAID uses to coordinate TCB efforts with other U.S. government agencies at home and abroad; and (3) describe how, if at all, USAID has used TCB evaluations in its program and project management. For fiscal years 2011 and 2012, we also identified the appropriations accounts from which USAID and State allocated funds for TCB-related activities and the obligations from these accounts for such activities (see app. I).

To address these objectives, we built upon information collected for our 2005 and 2011 reports on TCB and analyzed data from the U.S. government TCB database. Data from the TCB database were previously deemed reliable for our 2005 and 2011 reports on TCB. We identified limitations to the TCB database in our 2011 report on TCB, including that the database did not adequately explain significant factors driving changes in the composition of TCB funding over time. For this 2014 report on TCB, we assessed data from fiscal years 2008 through 2012 and determined that the data were sufficiently reliable to identify TCB funding by agency, country, and category.[1] Furthermore, in assessing the data, we interviewed key USAID officials and the contractor responsible for administering the database, and reviewed supporting documentation.

We primarily focused on TCB activities that USAID conducted because USAID provided the most funding of all U.S. agencies for TCB activities in 2012. However, we also sought the views of three other entities in our review regarding coordination with USAID on TCB activities: (1) the Department of State (State) because it is committed to supporting the negotiation and implementation of trade agreements and thereby helps countries advance trade initiatives; (2) the Millennium Challenge Corporation (MCC) because it conducts TCB-related activities that

---

[1]In 2011, we found that the U.S. government TCB database did not adequately explain significant factors driving changes in the composition of TCB funding over time or factors that underlie the increase in annual funding from $1.35 billion in 2005 to $1.69 billion in 2010. We recommended that USAID publicly report identified limitations and key distinctions in the categories of TCB assistance in the database. See GAO-11-727. In response to the recommendation, USAID streamlined and clarified the definitions of TCB categories to facilitate reporting and improve transparency. This change was reflected in the "technical notes" section of the TCB database. In addition, USAID noted on the TCB database website that, for many TCB activities in the database, the funding level does not match up with the fiscal year or years in which the activity is in operation or being funded.

support its broader strategic and agency mission goals, although it does
not have a specific TCB mission; and (3) the Office of the U.S. Trade
Representative (USTR) because of its role in leading trade efforts. In
conducting our work, we analyzed strategic, budget, and programmatic
documents describing these agencies' TCB-related funding and activities.
We also reviewed the 2010 TCB evaluation, along with evaluations and
assessments of TCB projects in the countries we visited. We conducted
fieldwork in Vietnam, Laos, Thailand, Ethiopia, Tanzania, and Kenya. We
selected these countries because they (1) had a cross-section of projects
that would allow us to compare and contrast different types of activities,
(2) are at different stages of economic development, (3) are in diverse
geographic regions, or (4) had signed an MCC compact and received
MCC-related TCB assistance. In each country, we analyzed agencies'
strategy, coordination, and program management efforts. We also
interviewed agency officials, host government officials, and contractors
implementing TCB activities in the field, and visited TCB project sites. Our
findings from these countries are not generalizable to the universe of all
USAID TCB activities.

To determine the extent to which USAID's 2003 strategy guides USAID's
TCB activities, we reviewed the strategy and relevant documents and
interviewed USAID officials in Washington, D.C.; Ethiopia; Kenya; Laos;
Tanzania; Thailand; and Vietnam about what they use to guide TCB
activities in their countries. We also interviewed these officials about the
agencies' TCB priorities and the relevance of the strategy to the current
environment. We reviewed guidance on strategic planning from several
sources, including USAID's internal policies, the Government
Performance and Results Act Modernization Act of 2010, and prior GAO
work on strategic planning, for criteria on updating strategies. We did not
review USAID's 2003 TCB strategy using the full set of six characteristics
of a national strategy that we identified in prior work; we determined that
many of the characteristics may not apply to it because it is only an
agency document and not a national strategy. However, in reviewing the
strategy we did examine the extent to which it reflected the current TCB
environment, because the strategy was developed over 10 years ago.
TCB environment refers to the context—including all conditions, entities,
events, and surrounding factors—in which agencies providing TCB
assistance are operating.

To describe methods USAID uses to coordinate TCB efforts with other
U.S. government agencies at home and abroad, we interviewed officials
from USAID, State, USTR, and MCC, and analyzed relevant documents.
During our fieldwork, we also spoke with officials from other agencies,

such as the U.S. Department of Agriculture and the Department of
Commerce, which in some cases play a role in TCB activities. We used
GAO's prior work on collaboration, which reports on collaboration
mechanisms and key practices for consideration, to develop our interview
questions for USAID and other agency officials, and to help identify
actions USAID has taken.[2] However, we did not formally assess USAID's
TCB coordination with other agencies.

To describe how, if at all, USAID has used TCB evaluations in its program
and project management, we interviewed officials from USAID and
analyzed relevant documents. During our fieldwork, we reviewed
evaluations and assessments of projects in the countries we visited. We
did not assess the challenges or effectiveness of TCB measurement and
evaluation processes in place because we addressed these issues in our
2011 report.[3]

We conducted this performance audit from October 2013 to August 2014
in accordance with generally accepted government auditing standards.
Those standards require that we plan and perform the audit to obtain
sufficient, appropriate evidence to provide a reasonable basis for our
findings and conclusions based on our audit objectives. We believe that
the evidence obtained provides a reasonable basis for our findings and
conclusions based on our audit objectives.

---

[2]GAO, *Managing for Results: Key Considerations for Implementing Interagency
Collaborative Mechanisms*, GAO-12-1022 (Washington, D.C.: Sept. 27, 2012); and GAO,
*Results-Oriented Government: Practices That Can Help Enhance and Sustain
Collaboration among Federal Agencies*, GAO-06-15 (Washington, D.C.: Oct. 21, 2005).

[3]GAO-11-727.

Appendix III: U.S. Government Trade Capacity Building Database and Definitional Categories

TCB Database

As we previously noted in 2011, the U.S. Agency for International Development (USAID) collects data to identify and quantify the U.S. government's trade capacity building (TCB) activities in developing countries through an annual survey of agencies on behalf of the Office of the U.S. Trade Representative (USTR), and oversees a contractor that collects and maintains the survey results in the U.S. government's publicly available online TCB database.[1] The data gathered from this survey are used to inform and respond to inquiries from Congress, the executive branch, the general public, and multilateral organizations such as the World Trade Organization (WTO). USTR officials use the database regularly and, according to these officials, it is a useful tool for identifying U.S. agencies' TCB activities and funding in a particular country or region, as well as the full extent of assistance the U.S. government provides in that area. In addition to administering this survey, USAID is also tasked with reviewing completed survey forms, and checking for accuracy and consistency in the reporting of funding and their allocation into TCB categories. A variety of U.S. agencies have a role in providing TCB assistance, including the Departments of State, the Army, Labor, the Treasury, and Commerce; the Millennium Challenge Corporation (MCC); and USAID.

TCB Category Definitions

USAID's survey asks agencies to place their TCB assistance into a range of categories and estimate funding obligated for each category. The U.S. government TCB database defines the categories as follows:

- WTO Accession and Compliance: Support for countries to benefit from membership in the WTO, or to understand fully the benefits of membership. Also assistance to help countries in the WTO accession process meet the requirements of accession. In addition, it includes assistance to meet the obligations of the specific WTO agreements, except for Agreements on Sanitary and Phyto-sanitary Measures (SPS), Technical Barriers to Trade (TBT), Intellectual Property Rights (IPR), and Trade-related Procurement. Those four agreements benefit from TCB in their own categories.
- Sanitary and Phyto-Sanitary Measures: Support for countries to meet SPS standards for trade and to comply with the WTO Agreement on SPS.

---

[1]See GAO-11-727, p. 4-5.

- Technical Barriers to Trade: Support for countries to reduce technical barriers to trade and to comply with the WTO Agreement on TBT.
- Intellectual Property Rights: Support for countries to observe international standards on intellectual property rights protection and to comply with the WTO Agreement on IPR.
- Trade-related Procurement: Support for increased trade related to government procurement and to comply with the WTO Agreement on Government Procurement.
- Trade Facilitation: Generally defined as assistance in lowering the costs of engaging in, or eliminating obstacles to international trade flows. Trade facilitation (for 2011) is a sum of the following four subcategories:

  - Customs Operations: Includes assistance to help countries modernize and improve their customs offices.
  - Trade Promotion: Includes assistance to increase market opportunities for developing country and transition economy producers.
  - Enterprise Development: Includes support to improve the associations and networks in the business sector, as well as to enhance the skills of business people engaged in trade. Also includes assistance to help countries acquire and use information technology to promote trade by creating business networks and disseminating market information.
  - FTAs and Trade Integration: Includes assistance to an FTA, an regional trade agreement, or to an individual country that increases the ability of the RTA to facilitate trade. It can also include assistance to a potential member of an RTA that improves the analytical capacity of the country's government with respect to RTA issues. (Note: It does not include TCB assistance in a specific area that is being provided to countries through an RTA. For example, technical assistance to help RTA member countries comply with SPS standards was reported as Trade-Related Agricultural Development or the WTO Agreement on SPS Measures.)

- Trade-related Labor: Assistance to support the enforcement of labor standards and worker rights, development of trade unions and dispute resolution mechanisms, strategies for workforce development and worker training, and the elimination of child labor.
- Financial Sector: Support for financial sector work, monetary and fiscal policy, exchange rates, commodity markets, and capital markets.

- Trade-related Infrastructure: Assistance to establish trade-related telecoms, transport, ports, airports, power, water, and industrial zones.
- Environmental Sector Trade and Standards: Assistance to establish environmental standards or to promote environmental technology.
- Competition Policy, Business Environment, and Governance: Support for the design and implementation of antitrust laws, as well as of laws and regulations related to investment and investor protections. Includes support for legal and institutional reform to improve governance and make policies more transparent, and assistance to help the different agencies of a host country government function more effectively in the trade policy arena.
- Trade-related Agriculture: Support for trade-related aspects of the agriculture and agribusiness sectors. (Note: Support that is specifically intended to help countries participate in the WTO Agreements on Agriculture or SPS Measures is not included in this category.)
- Trade-related Services: Includes support to help developing countries and transition economies increase their flows of trade in services. Services Trade Development is a sum of two subcategories:

  - Trade-related Services (excluding tourism): Assistance to help countries develop trade in services in all sectors other than tourism, including financial services, energy, transportation, and education.
  - Trade-related Tourism: Assistance to help countries expand their international tourism sectors, including eco-tourism.

- Other Trade Capacity Building: A small number of TCB activities did not fit in any of the above categories, including some activities of a crosscutting nature. These were categorized as "Other Trade Capacity Building."

Appendix IV: Comments from the Millennium Challenge Corporation

MILLENNIUM
CHALLENGE CORPORATION
UNITED STATES OF AMERICA

DATE: June 30, 2014

TO: Kimberly Gianopoulos
          Director
          International Affairs and Trade
          U.S. Government Accountability Office

FROM: Gina Porto Spiro
          Senior Director of Operations
          Department of Compact Operations
          Millennium Challenge Corporation

RE: MCC Comments on GAO draft report U.S. Trade Capacity Building Programs and
          Activities (GAO 321001)

This memorandum serves as the Millennium Challenge Corporation's (MCC) official comment
on the GAO "Foreign Assistance: USAID Should Update Its Trade Capacity Building Strategy"
draft report.

MCC has no comments on the report other than to note (as we have noted to GAO in connection
with GAO's recent audit #321017 on AGOA Trade) that MCC is in the process of updating the
MCC data in the USAID trade capacity building database.

If you have any questions, please contact Karla L. Chryar, MCC Compliance Officer at (202) 772-
6805 or chryarkl@mcc.gov.

875 Fifteenth Street NW | Washington, DC | 20005-2221 | p: (202) 521-3600 | f: (202) 521-3700 | www.mcc.gov

Appendix V: GAO Contact and Staff Acknowledgments

GAO Contact	Kimberly Gianopoulos, (202) 512-8612 or GianopoulosK@gao.gov
Staff Acknowledgments	In addition to the contact listed above, Juan Gobel (Assistant Director), Marc Castellano, Debbie Chung, Martin De Alteriis, Ernie Jackson, Michael Maslowski, and Oziel Trevino made key contributions to this report.

GAO's Mission	The Government Accountability Office, the audit, evaluation, and investigative arm of Congress, exists to support Congress in meeting its constitutional responsibilities and to help improve the performance and accountability of the federal government for the American people. GAO examines the use of public funds; evaluates federal programs and policies; and provides analyses, recommendations, and other assistance to help Congress make informed oversight, policy, and funding decisions. GAO's commitment to good government is reflected in its core values of accountability, integrity, and reliability.
Obtaining Copies of GAO Reports and Testimony	The fastest and easiest way to obtain copies of GAO documents at no cost is through GAO's website (http://www.gao.gov). Each weekday afternoon, GAO posts on its website newly released reports, testimony, and correspondence. To have GAO e-mail you a list of newly posted products, go to http://www.gao.gov and select "E-mail Updates."
Order by Phone	The price of each GAO publication reflects GAO's actual cost of production and distribution and depends on the number of pages in the publication and whether the publication is printed in color or black and white. Pricing and ordering information is posted on GAO's website, http://www.gao.gov/ordering.htm. Place orders by calling (202) 512-6000, toll free (866) 801-7077, or TDD (202) 512-2537. Orders may be paid for using American Express, Discover Card, MasterCard, Visa, check, or money order. Call for additional information.
Connect with GAO	Connect with GAO on Facebook, Flickr, Twitter, and YouTube. Subscribe to our RSS Feeds or E-mail Updates. Listen to our Podcasts. Visit GAO on the web at www.gao.gov.
To Report Fraud, Waste, and Abuse in Federal Programs	Contact: Website: http://www.gao.gov/fraudnet/fraudnet.htm E-mail: fraudnet@gao.gov Automated answering system: (800) 424-5454 or (202) 512-7470
Congressional Relations	Katherine Siggerud, Managing Director, siggerudk@gao.gov, (202) 512-4400, U.S. Government Accountability Office, 441 G Street NW, Room 7125, Washington, DC 20548
Public Affairs	Chuck Young, Managing Director, youngc1@gao.gov, (202) 512-4800 U.S. Government Accountability Office, 441 G Street NW, Room 7149 Washington, DC 20548

Please Print on Recycled Paper.

www.ingramcontent.com/pod-product-compliance
Lightning Source LLC
Chambersburg PA
CBHW080636290526
45790CB00007B/3094